BIOMES
of the World™

DECIDUOUS FORESTS

Seasons of Survival

Jeanne Nagle

rosen publishing's
rosen
central®

New York

To Dave, who would make the forest his home, if he could

Published in 2009 by The Rosen Publishing Group, Inc.
29 East 21st Street, New York, NY 10010

Copyright © 2009 by The Rosen Publishing Group, Inc.

First Edition

Library of Congress Cataloging-in-Publication Data

Nagle, Jeanne.
Deciduous forests : seasons of survival / Jeanne Nagle.—1st ed.
     p. cm.—(Biomes of the world)
Includes bibliographical references.
ISBN-13: 978-1-4358-5001-9 (library binding)
ISBN-13: 978-1-4358-5427-7 (pbk)
ISBN-13: 978-1-4358-5433-8 (6 pack)
1. Forest ecology—Juvenile literature. 2. Forests and forestry—Juvenile literature. I. Title.
QH541.5.F6 N34 2009
577.3—dc22

                                                                    2008022263

Manufactured in the United States of America

On the cover: Deciduous leaves changing color as autumn approaches.

CONTENTS

INTRODUCTION

There are hundreds of places on Earth that exist as small, individual worlds of their own. Scientists call these places ecosystems, or biomes. Within these special geographic areas live many different populations of plants and animals. Each resident is well suited to the weather and other environmental conditions of its biome, and each plays a role in keeping the ecosystem alive and healthy.

Biomes are either terrestrial, meaning that they are based on land, or aquatic, which means they are in water. Aquatic biomes are broken down into two groups: marine biomes and freshwater biomes. Marine biomes are found in the world's saltwater oceans. They can either be temperate, where the temperatures are neither too hot nor too cold, or they can be tropical, which means the oceans stay fairly warm because they are so near the equator. Freshwater biomes, the other kind of aquatic ecosystem, include rivers, streams, ponds, and lakes. Wetlands, which are made up of land that is soggy because it has water pooling in its top layers and sometimes over its surface, are also considered freshwater biomes.

Terrestrial biomes are split into even more categories: deserts, grasslands, tundra, and forests. Taking the

Although they look kind of deserted in the winter, forests—home to several species of plants and animals—are actually the most active and lively of the terrestrial biomes.

division a step further, forest biomes have three categories, which are rain forests, coniferous forests, and deciduous forests. Rain forests, located near the equator, are warm and moist all year round. Coniferous forests are found up north and in mountain areas, and they tend to have cold winters and short, cool summers. Deciduous forests have the best of everything—they experience all four seasons, and the temperatures don't get too warm or too cold at any given time of the year.

When it comes to ecology and environmental issues, scientists pay a great deal of attention to forests among the terrestrial biomes. This is because forests are the ecosystems that have the most animals and plants living in them, as well as the most biodiversity, which is a variety of species, or types, living in one place. The more species in an ecosystem, the more complex and interesting life in that ecosystem becomes.

Coniferous forests have pretty good biodiversity. But the largest number and most variety of plant and animal species can be found in the warm and moist tropical rain forests and the deciduous forests.

CHAPTER 1

ENTER THE DECIDUOUS FOREST

If you've ever been in a forest, then you know what makes it different from other ecosystems: the vegetation. Plentiful trees, bushes, and plants grow closely together across a large area in a forest.

All forests are created by a process known as succession. This begins when grass and small plants grow on a patch of bare land. This vegetation changes the condition of the soil, making it possible for bushes and trees to grow. Eventually, certain trees become dominant, or the main type of tree in the forest, because they are able to consume lots of moisture and nutrients before any other species has a chance to eat or drink.

That's how forests are similar. What separates the three kinds of forest biomes are the specific types of vegetation, especially trees, that grow in them.

Location and Classification

Technically, there are three types of deciduous forests: temperate, moist tropical, and dry tropical. Temperate deciduous forests are the ones that exist in the Northern Hemisphere, where there is a moderate climate (see chapter 2) and four seasons. These forests are found in the eastern third of the United States and the southern part of Canada, as well as in western Europe and

Temperate forests in North America are ablaze with color in the fall. The tallest, dominant trees tower over the other vegetation in the deciduous forest.

Asia (China, Korea, and Japan). Temperate deciduous trees include oaks, maples, beeches, and hickories. Chestnuts used to be a common hardwood in North America, but disease has practically wiped this species off the map.

Temperate deciduous forests are further classified by the main species, or types, of trees in them. For example, deciduous forests in North America are divided into categories such as beech-maple, maple-basswood, and oak-hickory. Areas where there is a generous mix of deciduous trees are called mesophytic forests.

Scattered throughout the world's Southern Hemisphere, tropical deciduous forests do not have four seasons and they pretty much stay warm all year round. Mexico, Venezuela, Columbia, India,

Madagascar, and Australia are some of the countries that are home to these forests. Deciduous trees in the Southern Hemisphere generally do not grow as tall as trees in northern temperate forests. Their trunks and branches also twist more, and their bark is thicker than that of temperate deciduous trees. Teaks, acacias, and rosewoods are some of the species of tropical deciduous trees.

Tropical forests are classified as either dry or moist. Dry tropical deciduous forests experience long periods with little or no precipitation. Moist tropical deciduous forests also have dry periods, but they are very short. Precipitation is commonplace in these areas.

Leaves are raked off lawns but lie undisturbed on the ground in forests, where they enrich the soil.

All About Leaves

The word "deciduous" is Latin for "to fall," which in the case of deciduous forests refers to the leaves on trees. Deciduous trees have broad, flat leaves that turn various colors as they die. They then fall off of branches before the cold winter months. (The leaves of dry tropical deciduous trees tend to fall off during their region's long, dry seasons.) This is the opposite of conifers, which have needles that stay on all year long, and trees in rain forests, which don't experience cool weather and, therefore, don't drop their leaves seasonally.

Leaves are how deciduous trees absorb sunlight, which helps turn water and carbon dioxide into food for trees through a process

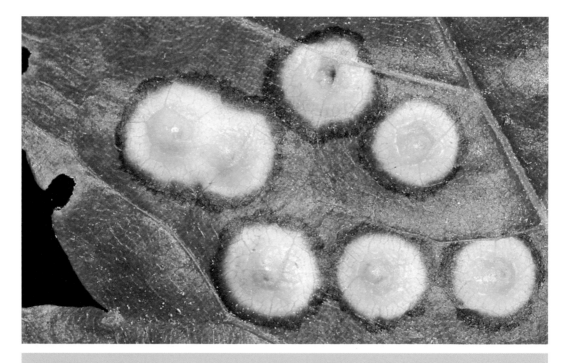

Autumn leaves may show signs of decay or disease, like the fungus on this maple leaf. When leaves fall, they protect trees from such conditions.

known as photosynthesis. Chlorophyll, a chemical produced during photosynthesis, is what makes leaves green. In the fall and winter, there is less sunlight and available water, so photosynthesis cannot occur. Without photosynthesis, the leaves lose chlorophyll and, as a result, their green color. The red, orange, yellow, and brown of autumn leaves are actually the color of unused food and water.

Falling leaves are also nature's way of protecting a tree. Without leaves, trees are better able to store the water they need to survive the winter inside their trunks, instead of doing what they would naturally do during warmer weather, which is spread nutrients and water out to all the leaves. Also, if the leaves stayed on the trees in cold temperatures, then the water stored in them would freeze. That would cause damage to the tree's entire system and leave it open to attacks by fungi, bacteria, and all sorts of diseases. For the most part, however, leaves fall off of trees because they have served their purpose and are no longer needed. Essentially, they get old and die after just one growing season.

Age, Height, and Weight

Leaves may not have long lives, but deciduous trees sure do. Several deciduous species have

Hardwood trees, like those found in the deciduous forest, can grow very tall and strong, surviving for hundreds of years.

existed for ages. The ginkgo, found in China, Europe, and North America, is thought to have been around for more than 260 million years—practically since the world began. Individual trees typically live anywhere from 100 to 250 years. Baobabs, which grow in Africa and other locations with tropical (hot and humid) climates, have been known to live thousands of years.

In theory, deciduous trees could live forever because they are able to grow indefinitely. Unlike humans, who reach a certain height and then stop, deciduous trees grow throughout their lives—not only up, but outward as well. During each growing season, which is six or seven months during the spring and summer, the trunks of deciduous trees get thicker as the trees get taller. The average

TELLTALE RINGS

As a tree grows each year, a fresh layer of vessels that carry food and water from the soil build up underneath the bark, making the trunk get thicker. Obvious start and finish marks that group the vessels together each year make it look as if there are rings in the wood. You can tell how old a tree is by counting its rings.

Growth rings also provide clues regarding weather conditions inside a deciduous forest over the years. When there are plenty of nutrients and water in the soil for a tree to absorb, lots of vessels form, making the rings thicker. Thinner rings indicate that growing conditions have been poor.

deciduous tree can grow up to 5 feet (1.5 meters) around and 80 to 100 feet (20 to 30 m) high.

Perhaps one of the reasons why deciduous trees live so long and grow so tall is that they are quite strong and hardy. All living things are made up of cells, which produce energy that allows life forms to survive and grow. The type of cells in a tree's trunk, and how closely they are packed together, helps determine whether a tree is deciduous or not. In addition to cells that carry water, which every tree has, deciduous trees have many fiber-filled cells, and there's not much space between any of the cells. This makes the wood of these trees heavy and solid. That is why deciduous trees are referred to as hardwoods. Almost all the trees in a deciduous forest are hardwoods.

Reproduction

Most deciduous trees have flowers that bloom in the spring. On some trees, like cherries, magnolias, and dogwoods, the blossoms are very apparent, while the flowers on trees such as the oak are small and not always visible.

These flowers make it possible for hardwoods to reproduce. Birds, bees, and other insects carry pollen between male and female flowers, which creates pollinated seeds contained in a nut or other protective covering. The seeds drop to the ground or are carried off by wind or animals, and then are buried in soil. There, they grow into seedlings, then saplings, and then mature trees.

Deciduous Forest Zones

There are several layers to the deciduous forest, called zones, which work their way from top to bottom. The tallest mature trees form

Sunlight often has a difficult time getting through the canopy of the deciduous forest. Leafy top branches grow close together, creating lots of shade down below.

what is called the canopy. This is where tree branches join together to form a roof over the rest of the forest. Oaks and hickories are generally responsible for the canopy of temperate deciduous forest biomes, while tropical locations have teak and sycamores rising to the top.

Next is the small tree and sapling zone, where young trees make their home. Typically, saplings are trees that don't mind the shade created by the canopy, and they can grow without a lot of sunlight. The same is true of the bushes in the shrub zone beneath the saplings. Some common deciduous shrubs include rhododendrons, azaleas, junipers, and laurels. Underneath the shrubs lies the herb zone, where short plants and, of course, herbs can be found.

Finally, there is the ground zone, also known as the forest floor. Living there are algae and fungi, including lichens and mushrooms, and several different kinds of moss that create a squishy carpet on the forest floor.

CHAPTER 2

THE DECIDUOUS ENVIRONMENT

Life in the temperate deciduous forest is never boring. Seasons change, causing leaves to turn color, flowers to bloom, and streams to ice over and then melt into action. The surface appearance of the biome's entire landscape fluctuates throughout the year. However, other aspects of the deciduous forest remain remarkably the same, month after month, year after year. These include the biome's overall climate, geography, and natural resources.

Reliably Mild

Because the weather in a deciduous forest is seasonal, meaning it changes with the seasons, you might not think there's much that is stable about the climate of this biome. Yet, there is one thing that you can rely on: temperatures will always be moderate, which means reasonable or somewhere in the middle.

In other words, the temperate deciduous forest gets warm but not overly hot in the summer, and cold but not too cold in the winter. Average summer temperatures are around 70 degrees Fahrenheit (20 degrees Celsius), but they can climb as high as the low-80s° F (high-20s° C). In winter, the thermometer doesn't go much above freezing (high-20s° C) or below 10° F (high-20s° C). Spring and fall are also pretty mild.

Whether it's four (summer, fall, winter, spring) or two (dry and wet), deciduous trees go through a lot of changes across the seasons.

Precipitation, which is moisture from rain or snow, is also fairly moderate yet plentiful. Anywhere from 30 to 80 inches (80 to 200 centimeters) at high-60s° F (high-20s° C), with a minimum of at least 20 inches (51 cm) at the same temperature, falls in the forest over the course of a year. The only other biome that gets more water in a year is the one with a form of precipitation in its name—the rain forest. In the deciduous forest, there is usually greater precipitation in the spring and summer than there is in the fall or winter. This works out perfectly because spring and summer are the growing season there. The plants and hardwood trees in the forest need plenty of water to help them grow.

OCEANS AND THE WEATHER

It is not by coincidence that temperate deciduous forest biomes are located near oceans. After all, biomes are defined mainly by their climate, and oceans have a great deal of influence over the weather.

The sun's rays warm the land and the water on Earth, but large bodies of water such as oceans do not absorb heat quickly. Most of the heat in oceans stays near the surface, within the first 1,300 feet (400 m). However, strong currents—streams of seawater driven primarily by the wind and gravity that stir the oceans—mix water of different temperatures together to make water temperature more even, or stable. As the oceans get warmer (thanks to currents), seawater evaporates and rises into the atmosphere, raising air temperatures and creating precipitation.

The Ups and Downs of Forest Geography

The topography, or physical characteristics of the land surface, can be very different from one deciduous forest to the next. In the past, vast hardwood forests had covered large, flat expanses of land, particularly in North America. The majority of deciduous forests on such plains, however, have been cleared to make way for agriculture. These days, most deciduous forests consist of tree-covered hills and valleys running along the countryside in the United States, Canada, western Europe, and Asia.

Mountains are also home to deciduous forests, at lower elevations. The climate changes higher up in the mountains, getting much

New York's Adirondack Mountains are high enough to support different types of deciduous trees, but not so high—and chilly—enough that conifers take over the landscape.

colder and drier to the point where deciduous trees are not able to survive. That type of weather is better suited to conifers, which are trees with needles instead of leaves. Pine, spruce, and fir are common kinds of conifers.

Wooded areas in the foothills, which are the lower parts of mountains, can have all broadleaf, hardwood trees. Deciduous trees have been known to scale mountains as high as 9,000 feet (2,743 m) above sea level, which is the scientific starting point for measuring the height of everything on Earth. The higher up the mountain, the more chance there is of encountering a mix of hardwoods and conifers.

Wet and Wild

By their nature, dry tropical forests do not have much access to water. Trees and other vegetation develop root systems that delve deep to gather groundwater, found in wells stored many feet below the surface of the forest floor. Temperate and moist tropical deciduous forests have an easier time getting water. In addition to precipitation, these areas have access to rivers and streams. Temperate forests may also contain lakes, ponds, and freshwater springs.

Along the shores of these rivers and streams, you might come across wetlands. Wetlands are areas of land that stay wet on or near the surface because the water cannot be absorbed into the ground. When the overflow is more seasonal, from rain and melted snow in the spring, floodplain forests can occur. Hardwood trees and vegetation that are able to survive weeks, even months, of flooding grow here. Floodplain forests and wetlands act as natural dams because they store and slow the flow of excess water, thereby protecting land that is downstream from damaging floods.

Rich, Fertile Soil

The floors of deciduous forests contain some of the best soil on Earth. That is because hardwood forests are great at recycling. Trees take food and water from the soil through their roots. Nutrients left in leaves when they fall to the ground are absorbed back into the soil as the leaves decompose, or rot naturally. They get a little help in this process from bacteria and earthworms, which eat and digest the dead vegetation and then excrete out an even richer form of soil known as humus. Large amounts of chemicals that help plants grow, like nitrogen, are present in humus.

Nutrients aren't the only valuable resources found in the soil of deciduous forests. Hidden deep within the earth, beneath the lush

The colorful foliage on the floor of temperate deciduous forests winds up giving back essential nutrients to the trees the dead leaves used to call home.

vegetation, are minerals that humans need and desire. Coal, which is a fuel source for heating and energy, can be found underground in North American and German deciduous forests. Gold is often discovered buried beneath tropical deciduous forests in places such as Madagascar, an island nation off the coast of Africa.

There's one more priceless resource that comes from the forest soil—the trees themselves. Strong hardwoods are the preferred materials when humans build houses and furniture. More than that, deciduous trees provide a habitat, or home, for many wild plants and animals.

CHAPTER 3

FOREST PLANTS AND ANIMALS

With a temperate climate, plenty of food and water, and adequate shelter, deciduous forest biomes are like paradise for all sorts of plants and animals. In fact, the deciduous forest is second only to the rain forest when it comes to biodiversity. Biodiversity is a great number and variety of species in one biome. Biodiversity is important because it takes various species interacting with each other to keep the world's biomes alive and healthy.

Seasons Full of Plants

Throughout the spring and summer growing seasons, plants of the temperate deciduous forest unfold like a Japanese fan. It's as if the vegetation takes turns, making sure that there is always some kind of greenery around.

In the spring, when trees are starting to sprout new leaves, lilies, primroses, bluebells, and other low-lying wildflowers start to blossom. Like deciduous trees, some plants (anemones and skunk cabbage) in the forest flower, while others, like various kinds of grasses and herbs, don't. Many of the early flowering plants die off once tree limbs are covered with broad leaves because less sunlight reaches them through the full canopy.

With trees sprouting new leaves and wildflowers blooming, spring brings rebirth to deciduous forests.

Summer is the time for plants that tolerate, or accept and deal with, shade. In the deciduous forest, these include ferns, ivy, and the carpet of moss on the forest floor. (Contrary to how it looks, moss is not a sheet of vegetation. It is made up of tiny, individual plants that huddle together.) Shrubs, such as witch hazel and sumac, are also full and leafy throughout the summer growing season.

Plants do appear during the growing season in tropical climates as well, except that plant growth is limited to the rainy season only.

In dry tropical forests, the rainy season could be as little as three months. That doesn't give plants much time to grow, so there isn't much vegetation other than trees in this particular biome. Small palms, a few hardy shrubs, and cacti—all of which don't need much water to survive—are the most typical plants in the dry tropical deciduous forest.

Moist tropical deciduous forests spend most of the year in rain, but there are dry seasons in these locations, too. Here, you will find "exotic" shrubs and plants such as flame bushes, indigofera, Herald's Trumpets, and microstegium. The last item in that list is a type of grass or weed.

Annuals and Perennials

In the autumn, as leaves change colors and drop off of the trees, deciduous forest plants also start to wither and die in preparation for the upcoming winter. Some will return in the spring, while others will not. The deciduous forest contains plants that are perennials, meaning they stick around for at least a couple of years, and annuals, which only have a one-year lifespan. Annuals do reproduce, however, so each particular kind of plant grows in the spring, just not the original plant that was there the year before.

The roots of deciduous trees often reach far underground to gather water and nutrition.

Just as trees protect themselves by stopping the flow of chlorophyll to leaves, deciduous perennial plants go through a process called hardening. This is when carbohydrates, which are a plant's food, collect in stems and leaves, making them firm instead of soft and flexible. The buildup of carbohydrates slows the plant's growth so that it can go dormant, or become inactive and rest, during the cold of winter, saving its energy for when it comes back in the spring.

Perennials in tropical climates don't need to prepare for the cold, so they don't go through hardening. But they do need to get ready for the dry season. Storing water is most important to plants in the dry tropical deciduous forest. Some plants have specially designed root systems that allow them to either gather groundwater deep under the forest floor or hold water like a vase for slow and steady

Raccoons exhibit several individual traits that belong to deciduous forest animals. They eat both plants and meat, and they sleep—but do not hibernate—during the winter.

use. Others have thorns or needles to keep animals away from the fluid they store in their stems and leaves.

Herbivores and Carnivores

Plant life in the deciduous forest is also an important food source for many of the animals that live in the biome. Creatures that eat leaves, grasses, and other vegetation are called herbivores. Many birds, which eat berries and seeds from plants, fall into this category. So do several smaller mammals, such as rabbits and squirrels. Larger, slower animals and those that have hooves also tend to be plant-eaters. Deer in temperate areas, zebras and gazelles in the dry tropics, and elephants in moist tropics are some of the animals that graze, or eat, vegetation in deciduous forests.

All of these creatures are herbivores because they are not built to hunt. Small mammals do not have the size or strength that it takes to overpower prey, large ones often don't have the speed or agility (quickness) to chase or catch anything, and claws are better than hooves when it comes to killing a meal.

The deciduous forest biome also has its share of carnivores, which are meat-eaters. They eat other animal inhabitants of the forest. Each class of animal—insects, arachnids, birds, amphibians, reptiles, and mammals—has its share of carnivores. Temperate forest carnivores include caterpillars, spiders, foxes, hawks, owls, wolves, and bobcats. It's the same story in tropical climates, only the species are different. Civets, which look like a cross between a cat and an otter, are some of the more exotic tropical deciduous forest carnivores. One of the most popular and well-known meat-eaters in the moist tropical deciduous forest is the tiger.

Plants are still important to carnivores because they provide a food source for the animals the carnivores eat. Without plants, the

NEITHER HERE NOR THERE

There are other life forms in the deciduous forest that are not classified as animals or plants. Algae make their own food through photosynthesis, like plants do, but they are considered protists, which is a catch-all term for living organisms that don't fit neatly into one category. Blue-green algae are common on land in the woods, although most algae form in water sources, like lakes and ponds.

Fungi, the plural of fungus, have similarities to both plants and animals, but they are neither. They live underground or in the cells of plants. Humans are used to seeing their blossoms or "fruit," what we call mushrooms. Fungi either soak up nutrients from dead or decaying matter such as dead leaves on the forest floor, or they attach themselves to living organisms and feed off of them. That's why you may see groups of mushrooms growing out of the base of a tree trunk.

carnivores' food supply would disappear. This is an example of biome interdependence.

In the deciduous forest biome, there are also omnivores. These are creatures that will eat both plants and meat. Temperate deciduous omnivores include raccoons and black bears. In fact, while bears will eat fish, ants, and grubs, the bulk of their diet consists of vegetation.

Winter Adaptations

Winter in the temperate deciduous forest is considered downtime. With cold temperatures, fewer hours of sunlight, the land covered in snow, and water sources iced over, this biome becomes a tough place for plants and animals to survive. Nature solves this problem through a process known as adaptation.

To "adapt" means to get used to something, or change so that a situation better fits your needs. Wild plants and animals adapt their behavior to live in the forest in winter. For instance, many plants become dormant, or inactive, when the temperature gets cold. One example of this is trees dropping their leaves.

Some animals hibernate, which is a form of dormancy. Hibernation is when a creature's body temperature drops, as does its heart rate. This state of relaxation is so deep that it's almost as if the animal is sleeping through the winter. Nourishment during hibernation is provided by either fat stored in an animal's body or collected supplies that the animal wakes up long enough to eat, then goes back to rest.

Migration is another seasonal adaptation. This is when groups of animals temporarily move to a habitat that has better food, shelter, and/or climate. Several species of birds and fish migrate from the forest in the fall, seeking warmer weather, only to return in the spring.

CHAPTER 4

THREATS TO THE DECIDUOUS FOREST

There used to be a lot more deciduous forests in the world than there are now. Most of Europe, half of North America, and large sections of Asia were dedicated to great stands of hardwood trees, as well as to the plants and animals that called them home. Now, fewer deciduous forests spot the landscape in these locations, rather than cover them. What's more, a majority of the forests that are still in existence are second-growth, or the next generation. Most of the original deciduous forest biome was destroyed, and smaller versions with younger trees sprang up in its place.

So, what ruined the old-growth deciduous forests? Disease was undeniably a factor. Chestnut trees used to be the dominant tree in the North American deciduous forest biome. In the 1800s, however, a fungal disease known as chestnut blight, which attacks a tree's roots and rots them away, virtually wiped out this entire species. In the United States today, the only evidence of chestnut trees is in the forest understory, as tiny sprouts that spring up from diseased stumps. Other hardwoods suffered a drastic decline as well. They were the victims of butternut canker, which destroys tree branches and stems, and Dutch elm disease, which affects the bark and moves in toward the trunk.

Although disease played a part, the destruction of deciduous forests has mainly been the result of human activity. Farming, development, logging, mining, and pollution have taken an awful toll on broadleaf forests around the world. The worst part is many of these threats remain active to this day.

Farming and Development

One of the deciduous forest's greatest assets has also turned out to be one of its biggest trouble areas: the biome's rich soil. The nitrogen in the soil is not only good for trees and plants, but it's also good for growing food crops. Farmers who settled near deciduous forests discovered this a long time ago.

This rotting tree is a victim of chestnut blight. Disease can wipe out entire species of trees.

People have been cutting down deciduous trees for farmland for close to four thousand years in China, hundreds of years in Europe, and since the 1600s in the United States.

Even sadder than losing forests is the fact that converting the land into farms eventually ruins the soil as well. The soil is so rich in the first place because of all the nutrients it absorbs from falling tree leaves and decomposing vegetation. Without the trees and plants of the deciduous forest, the land loses its fertility. After years of use for agriculture, nutrients in the soil are depleted, or used up, and farmers are forced to use unnatural chemicals to grow their crops.

Deciduous forests have been cleared for development, which is when humans change the land in the hopes of making it more valuable—to them. Cities, towns, homes, commercial buildings, and

Increased human population means that more land is being developed. Wooded areas are completely cleared of trees and are replaced by roads, homes, and other buildings.

roads are some of the developments that have taken the place of many forests.

As the world's population increases, so does the need for more living space, as well as farms to feed more people. This could mean the destruction of even more deciduous forests.

Logging and Mining

Development is actually a double whammy for the deciduous forest. Most homes, stores, and offices are built using lumber, which is the wood from trees. It is possible that trees could be removed from a forest, only to reappear on the cleared land in the form of wood-frame houses, hardwood floors, and wood furniture.

The rising demand for hardwood lumber—not to mention wood pulp used to make paper products—has caused an increase in cutting down forest trees, which is known as logging. According to David Boyd, director of Canada's environmental law organization Ecojustice, the practice of logging has doubled since 1950. The cheapest way to log is clear cutting, which is when several acres of trees are cut down, or felled, at once. All types of logging leave scars on the land in the form of dead stumps and bare, dug-up soil. But clear cutting is the worst.

Slurry, a result of strip mining, can pollute soil and bury trees. That's what happened in this Ohio valley.

Logging also leaves many deciduous forest animals without homes or a source of food. When trees and plants are gone, the soil gets loose and can wash away in the rain or wind. This is known as erosion, a process that devastates the quality of the biome's nutrient-rich soil. Without good soil, it's harder for the deciduous forest to make a comeback after extensive logging.

Other valuable resources can be found in the ground of deciduous forests, mainly coal. Mining, or digging deeply into the soil after clearing the area of trees, is necessary to get coal out of the ground. Strip mining, where large pits are cut into the land, is a cheap way to extract coal. Today, miners also use extremely powerful explosives to blast away complete forested mountain peaks in what's called

HAZARDOUS TO HUMANS, TOO

Trees, plants, and wild animals are not the only ones hurt by mining in the deciduous forest. In 2006, researchers at Eastern Kentucky University discovered that many children living near mining operations in Appalachia suffered from "blue baby syndrome," which causes nausea, vomiting, and shortness of breath. Minerals from the mines that leaked into drinking water were blamed. These minerals can also cause organ failure, bone damage, and cancer.

mountaintop removal. This leaves huge, bare patches of damaged soil and holes that can never be filled. It would take years for mined land to grow back into a forest—if ever.

Pollution and Global Warming

Mining pollutes the entire forest biome. Layers of dirt, rocks, and uprooted vegetation are dumped as solid waste, left in piles, or shoved down into valleys in mountain regions. Forest streams are filled in with unearthed dirt or turn black with slurry, which is the mineral runoff from coal mining and processing.

The machinery used in logging and mining releases exhaust fumes that contribute to the worldwide problem of climate change, also called global warming. Toxic chemicals from burning fossil fuels, such as gasoline and coal, build up in Earth's atmosphere and trap the sun's heat. This raises the planet's overall temperature and leads to other weather-related issues.

Acid rain, which is precipitation that is polluted by excess sulfur and nitrogen, can eat away at a tree. Human activity is the main cause of acid rain.

Changes in the amount of precipitation, rising temperatures altering the length of the growing season, and an increase in the number of forest fires are all consequences of global warming. These conditions can cause stress to hardwood trees.

Carbon dioxide and other gases that contribute to global warming are given off not only by equipment used in logging and mining. Driving automobiles, running factories, and other human activity emits, or releases into the air, these dangerous chemicals as well. This means that people can live nowhere near a deciduous forest and still be a threat to its existence.

CHAPTER 5

THE FUTURE OF THE FOREST

Because of past land conversion to agricultural and other development use, as well as mining and logging, many of the world's deciduous forests have gotten smaller or have disappeared altogether. Today, the broadleaf forests that remain are being threatened by a number of factors, both human-made and natural. So, what does the future hold for this biome? That will depend, in large part, on what humans choose to do or not do.

Why Saving Forests Is Important

Every living thing on Earth plays a role in keeping the planet healthy and able to support life. Among the services that the world's forests provide are cleaning the air and water, making the soil rich in nutrients, pollinating crops for food, reducing the number of pests and diseases that can cause harm, and keeping the climate stable.

The trees of the deciduous forest have plenty of these tasks to keep them busy. In addition to providing food and shelter, they produce oxygen and filter carbon dioxide and other harmful pollutants out of the air. In this way, they reduce the effects of global warming and leave the air safer to breathe.

Walls of trees can act as exhaust filters near schools by directing the heated aerosol of toxic particles up and dispersing the plume.

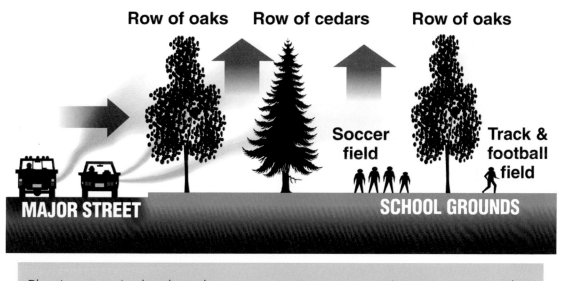

Planting trees in developed areas serves two purposes. It restores a natural balance, partially replacing trees that were cut down, and it helps filter pollution out of the air.

Hardwoods filter pollutants such as phosphorus out of the soil before they enter rivers and streams and other waterways. This is important because in the United States alone, more than half of the population drinks water from sources that originate in woodlands. When groups of trees stand together, they also keep the nutrient-rich forest soil in place so that erosion does not occur. Erosion allows dirt and silt to gather in rivers and streams, which spoils sources of freshwater.

Management, Conservation, and Restoration

The best way to make sure that deciduous forests have a future is through forest management. This involves taking action—and

Forest management doesn't mean making wooded areas totally off-limits. Conservation methods allow for stockpiling wood, but only as much as is needed—not to excess.

sometimes stepping aside and letting Mother Nature handle things—in order to keep the biome healthy and in balance.

Forest management is a system, like a set of rules or laws, which defines how the resources of the forest will be used. Decisions must be made about how much, if any, of the wooded land should be used for commercial purposes such as logging and mining, or recreation, like when a forest is designated a national park or hiking trails are set up among the trees. Another consideration is whether forests should be protected as natural habitats for plants and animals.

After deciding how the land should be used, management techniques are put in place by governments and private landowners, depending on who owns the forestland. The system must balance the needs of various cultures to use the resources of the forest (wood, coal, etc.) for their survival, or a way to earn a living, with the needs of wildlife and the health of the biome and planet. This is called sustainable development, which is based on the idea that humans shouldn't take more than they need from the environment.

Conservation is an example of forest management. This means protecting what already exists in the forest. To be successful, con-servation requires planning and goals, in both the long and short term. Conservationists should take a look at an individual forest's assets, place potential problem areas in order of importance and most urgent need, and act only after consideration of all the options, weighing the benefits for now and in the future.

Steps toward conservation include limits on logging and mining, taking extra precautions to stop fires from starting or spreading, finding ways to reduce diseases and pests, and conducting regular soil and water testing.

Restoration involves trying to bring the forest back to its original, natural state. In a way, it's the opposite of forest management because humans don't so much manage the forest as guide and assist it in its recovery, then step aside and let nature take its course. Helping deciduous forests restore themselves takes time. It takes years for young trees to grow into mature hardwoods. Patience and commitment are needed when it comes to restoration.

Hope for the Future

Many people, particularly those in the United States and other developed countries, have begun to see and understand how human activity can negatively affect the environment. Armed with this knowledge, they have started to take steps toward saving the

By promoting smart choices and raising awareness, conservation programs in China and around the world ensure the future of Earth's deciduous forests.

forests and other biomes that we still have and restoring the ones that have been ruined.

The United States has a long history of protecting forest biomes. As early as 1876, the country developed a Division of Forestry, which later became the Bureau of Forestry, designed to conserve and manage the nation's forests. President Theodore Roosevelt expanded the role of the bureau when he formed the U.S. National Forest Service in the early 1900s. Today, the Forest Service, as well as the Agriculture and Interior departments of the U.S. government, work to conserve, manage, and protect the country's forests. Protected areas usually take the form of either reserves or national parks.

Of the other nations that have deciduous forest biomes, China stands out as a leader in forest protection. The country is investing the equivalent of $11 billion in its National Forest Protection Program, which expects to protect millions of acres of forests, reduce logging and wood consumption, and find new employment for forest workers who lose their jobs because of all these changes.

There are also several nongovernmental organizations around the world that are working to secure a bright future for hardwood forests. Groups such as the Sierra Club and Nature Conservancy have pur- chased land and pushed for greater legal protection of public and privately owned forests. As long as initiatives like these come along, the future looks promising for the deciduous forest biome.

GLOSSARY

adapt To make a good fit; to get used to.

biome A large geographic region with a fairly predictable and consistent climate that supports specific plants and animals.

carnivorous Meat-eating.

chlorophyll A chemical in plants and trees that turns soil nutrients into food and turns leaves green.

conifer A tree with needles instead of leaves, cones instead of flowers.

conservation To save from loss, damage, or neglect.

currents Streams of seawater that stir the world's oceans.

deciduous The Latin word for "to fall"; refers to leaves falling off trees after a forest's growing season.

dominant The predominant, or main, type.

dormant Describing when perennial plants seem to die, only to come alive again when the weather gets warmer.

felled When a tree is cut down during logging.

floodplain forests Where hardwood trees and vegetation that can survive weeks, even months, of flooding grow.

forest management A system of rules/laws that determine how the resources of forests can and will be used.

habitat A home for wild animals and plants.

hibernate To go into a period of rest during the winter.

humus A super-rich form of soil made from the excrement (waste matter) of bacteria and insects.

mesophytic forest A mix of several species of deciduous trees.

migrate To move location from time to time, especially as the seasons change.

photosynthesis The process by which water is turned into food for plants and trees.

precipitation Water that falls from the sky in the form of rain, snow, sleet, or hail.

sapling A young, small tree.

species A type or category of animal or plant.

succession The process by which one type of tree is replaced by other stronger types of trees until there is one dominant tree in a forest.

temperate Moderate, or reasonable, and in the middle.

topography The physical characteristics of a land surface.

Canadian Parks and Wilderness Society
880 Wellington Street, Suite 506
Ottawa, ON K1R 6K7
Canada
(613) 569-7226
Web site: http://www.cpaws.org
With a network of thirteen chapters, the nonprofit CPAWS
helps to conserve Canada's most treasured wild places in
parks and other protected areas.

Ecojustice
131 Water Street, Suite 214
Vancouver, BC V6B 4M3
Canada
(800) 926-7744
Web site: http://www.ecojustice.ca
As Canada's largest and foremost nonprofit environmental law
organization, Ecojustice goes to court over environmental
issues, setting powerful precedents for clean water, natural
spaces, healthy communities, and global warming solutions.

Global Forest Watch
10 G Street NE
Washington, DC 20002
(202) 729-7600
Web site: http://www.globalforestwatch.org/english/index.htm
A division of the World Resources Institute, Global Forest
Watch is an international partnership that oversees forest
management and conservation efforts in regions that
are home to many of the world's most important forest
ecosystems.

Sierra Club
85 Second Street, 2nd Floor
San Francisco, CA 94105
(415) 977-5500
Web site: http://www.sierraclub.org
The Sierra Club works to protect local communities, eco-regions, and the planet as a whole through conservation, activism, and education. The organization has a national chapter in Canada as well.

U.S. Department of Agriculture Forest Service
1400 Independence Avenue SW
Washington, DC 20250-0003
(800) 832-1355
Web site: http://www.fs.fed.us
The USDA Forest Service manages public lands in national forests and grasslands, including boreal forests in Alaska.

Web Sites

Due to the changing nature of Internet links, Rosen Publishing has developed an online list of Web sites related to the subject of this book. This site is updated regularly. Please use this link to access the list:

http://www.rosenlinks.com/biom/deci

FOR FURTHER READING

Baldwin, Carol. *Living in a Temperate Deciduous Forest.* New Market, ON: Heinemann, 2003.

Fink Martin, Patricia A. *Woods and Forests: Exploring Ecosystems.* Danbury, CT: Franklin Watts, 2000.

Kirkland, Jane. *Take a Tree Walk.* Lionville, PA: Stillwater Publishing, 2002.

MacMillan, Dianne M. *Life in a Deciduous Forest.* Minneapolis, MN: Lerner Publishing Group, 2003.

Morton Cowan, Mary. *Timberrr . . . A History of Logging in New England.* Brookfield, CT: Millbrook Press, 2003.

Pulley-Sayre, April. *Temperate Deciduous Forests.* Brookfield, CT: Twenty-First Century Books, 1997.

Benders-Hyde, Elizabeth, and Karl Nelson. "Blue Planet Biomes." November 2006. Retrieved April 2008 (http://www.blueplanetbiomes.org/deciduous_forest.htm).

Boyd, David. "The Race to Save the World's Forests." Ecojustice. Retrieved April 2008 (http://www.fanweb.org/patrick-moore/dboyd.html).

Butcher, Brandon. "Seasons." CBS3 Springfield, March 2007. Retrieved April 2008 (http://www.cbs3springfield.com/weather/classroom/guidetometerology/6552032.html).

MacDougall, Andrew, and Judy Loo. "Natural History of the Saint John River Valley Hardwood Forest of Western New Brunswick and Northeastern Maine." Canadian Forest Service Atlantic Forestry Centre. Retrieved April 2008 (http://www.lib.unb.ca/Texts/Forest/MX204/English/MX204E.html).

Schlarbaum, Scott E., et al. "Three American Tragedies: Chestnut Blight, Butternut Canker, and Dutch Elm Disease." U.S. Department of Agriculture Forest Service. Retrieved April 2008 (http://www.srs.fs.usda.gov/pubs/ja/ja_schlarbaum002.htm).

U.S. Department of Commerce and Consumer Affairs. "Terrestrial Vegetation of the Virgin Islands." Retrieved April 2008 (http://www.vifishandwildlife.com/Education/FactSheet/DCCAFactSheets/PDFs/3Terrestrialvegetation.pdf).

Washington Department of Fish and Wildlife. "Living with Wildlife: Black Bears." Retrieved April 2008 (http://wdfw.wa.gov/wlm/living/bears.htm).

INDEX

About the Author

Jeanne Nagle is the author of several books on the natural world, including Rosen's *Extreme Environmental Threats: Wildlife* and *Biomes of the World: Coniferous Forests.*

Photo Credits

Designer: Les Kanturek; Editor: Nicholas Croce
Photo Researcher: Amy Feinberg